CARTER OOSTERHOUSE

A BIG Problem

Pictures by Chris Lensch

First published by Experience Early Learning Company
7243 Scotchwood Lane, Grawn, Michigan 49637 USA

ISBN: 978-1-937954-26-0
visit us at **www.ExperienceEarlyLearning.com**

CARTER OOSTERHOUSE

A BIG Problem

Pictures by Chris Lensch

There once was an elephant.

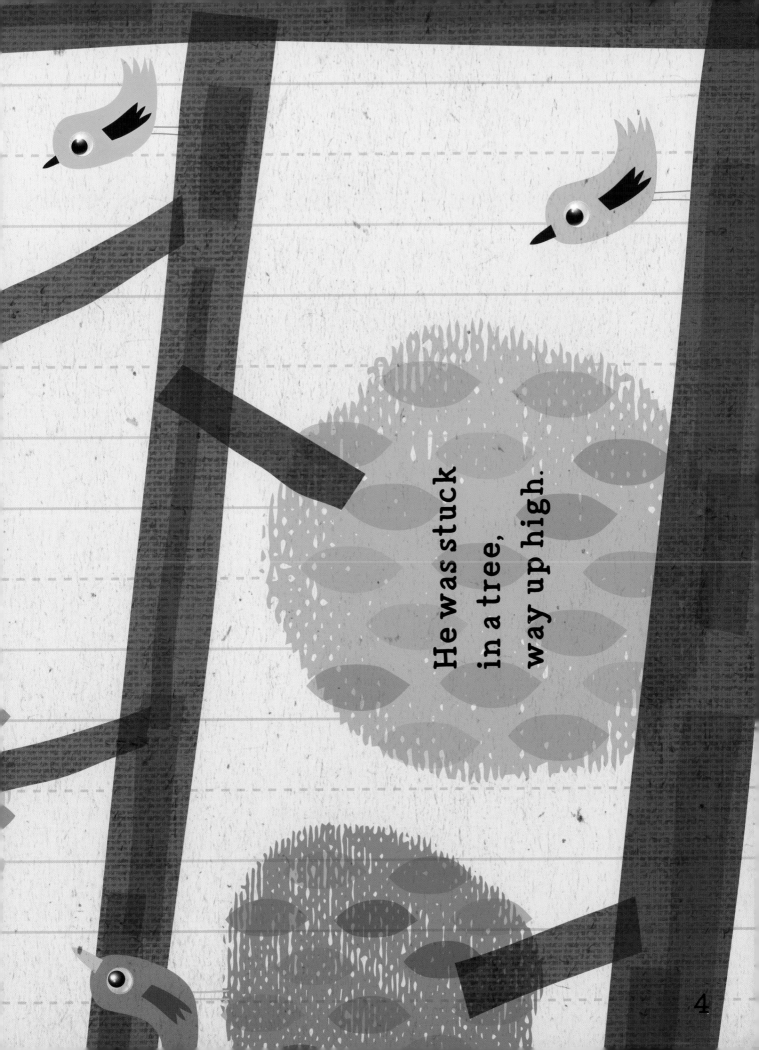

He was stuck in a tree, way up high.

4

"You should build something!"
said Mr. Carter. "We can start with
some ideas."

What can we make that is as tall as a tree?

Fire truck ladders?

Skyscrapers are tall!

A staircase...

9

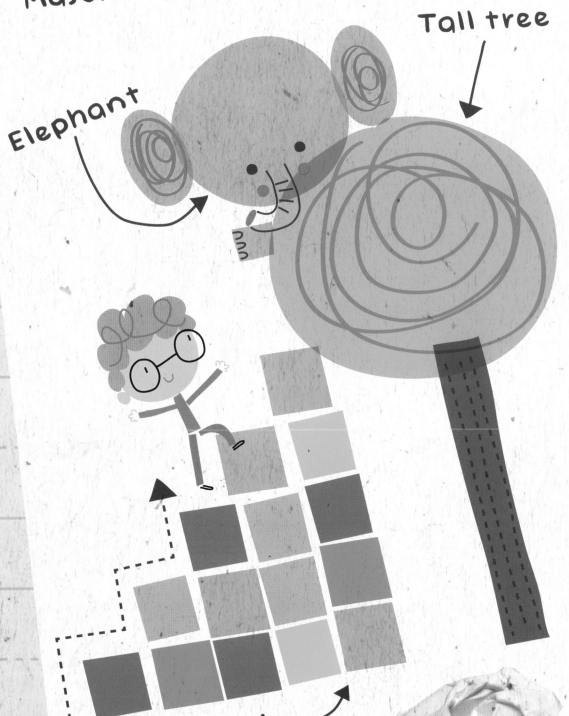

Mason's rescue plan - Version 2.0

Tall tree

Elephant

Block stairs

Version 1.0 →

The stairs worked perfectly for Mason,
but the elephant was worried.
They looked too wobbly for his big feet.

11

"Nice try!" said Mr. Carter, "but it looks like we will need to build something more stable."

What can we make that is tall and sturdy?

A bridge!

A ladder!

Another tree?

14

"These wires will make a terrific tower of triangles!" He announced.

Jungle Gym Rescue
by Luis

Tree branch

Jungle gym

Luis

Elephant

Unfortunately, elephants do not like climbing on jungle gyms as much as children do.

What if his foot slips between the bars!

18

"We're getting closer," said Mr. Carter. "Don't give up!"

What can we make that is tall, sturdy and has no holes?

A sandwich?

An airplane!

I'm hungry!

A rocket!

"I think perhaps we should engineer a pendulum!" said Anika.

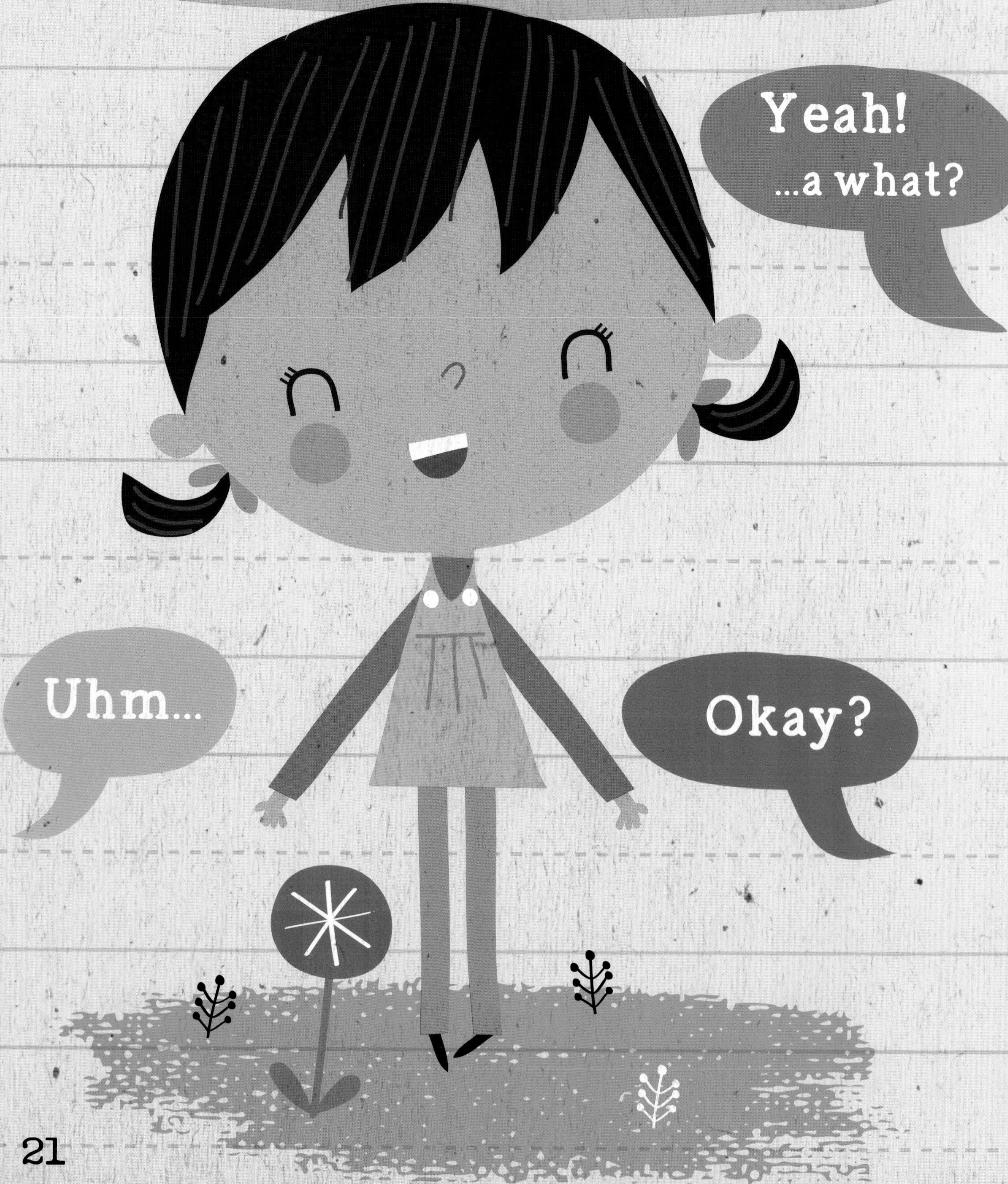

A Swing!

Me

Elephant

A simple swing
by Anika

The swing flew high and had a sturdy seat, but it was too fast for the elephant.

24

"Impressive," said Mr. Carter, "but we are not quite there."

What can we build that is tall, sturdy, has no holes and can stop at the top?

An elevator?

A crane?

How about...

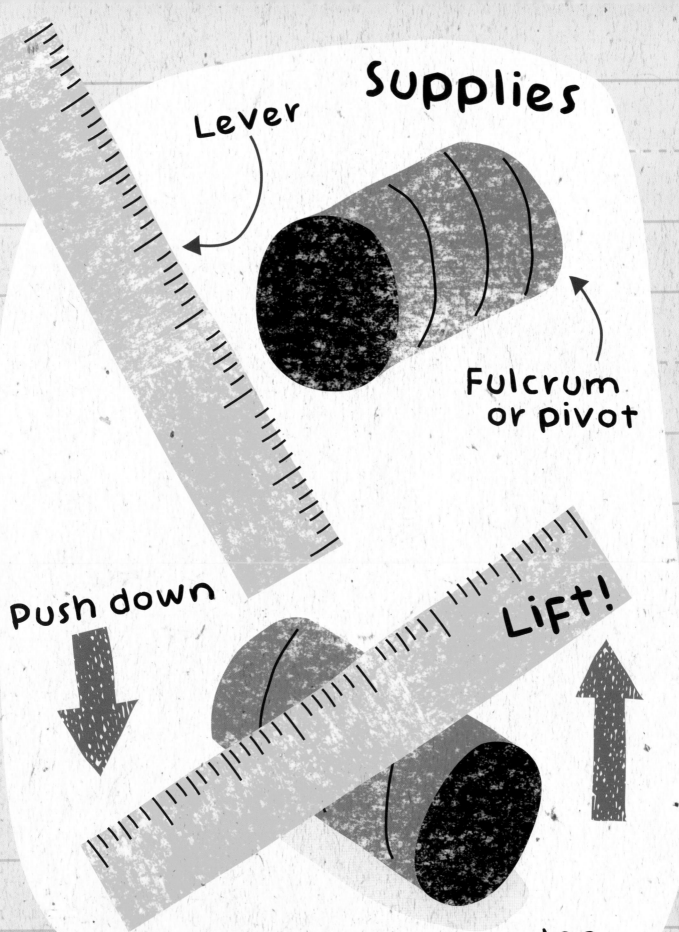

Supplies

Lever

Fulcrum or pivot

Push down

LIFT!

Chloe's super awesome plan

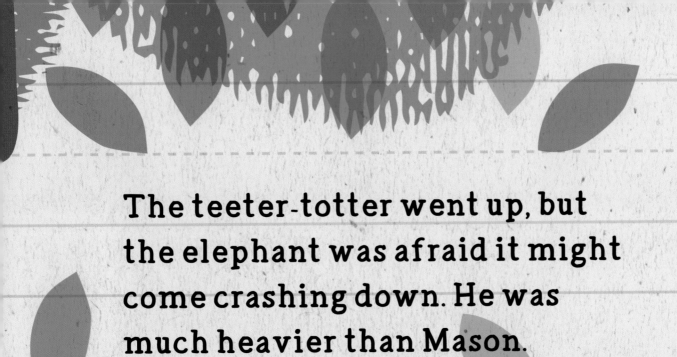

The teeter-totter went up, but the elephant was afraid it might come crashing down. He was much heavier than Mason.

"We will never get him down," said the children.

The elephant was very sad.

"We have worked so hard!" said Mr. Carter.

"Alone, you each had a great idea. What do you think might happen if you all worked together?"

What can we build together that is tall, sturdy, has no holes, stops at the top and can support a heavy elephant?

Let's make a slide!

35

36

Climb up

Pencils

Pipe Cleaners

<u>Our</u> super awesome plan

Slide down

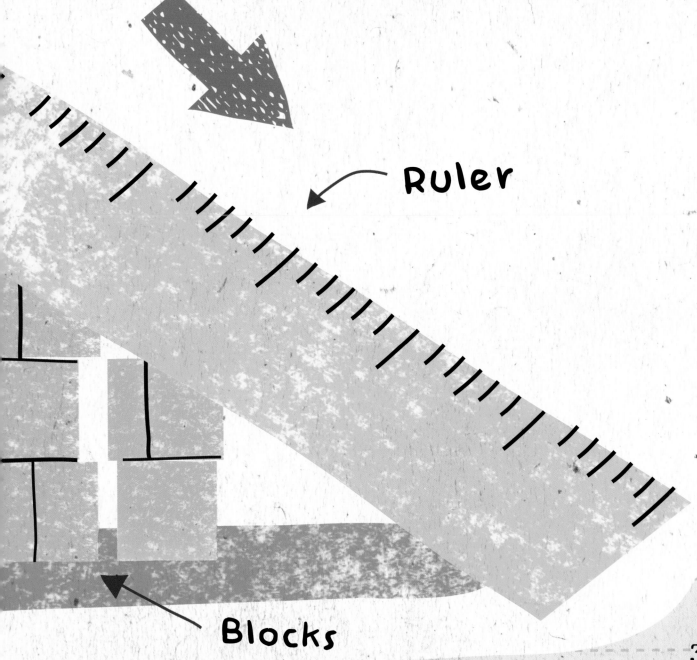

Ruler

Blocks

What should we do now?

Play!

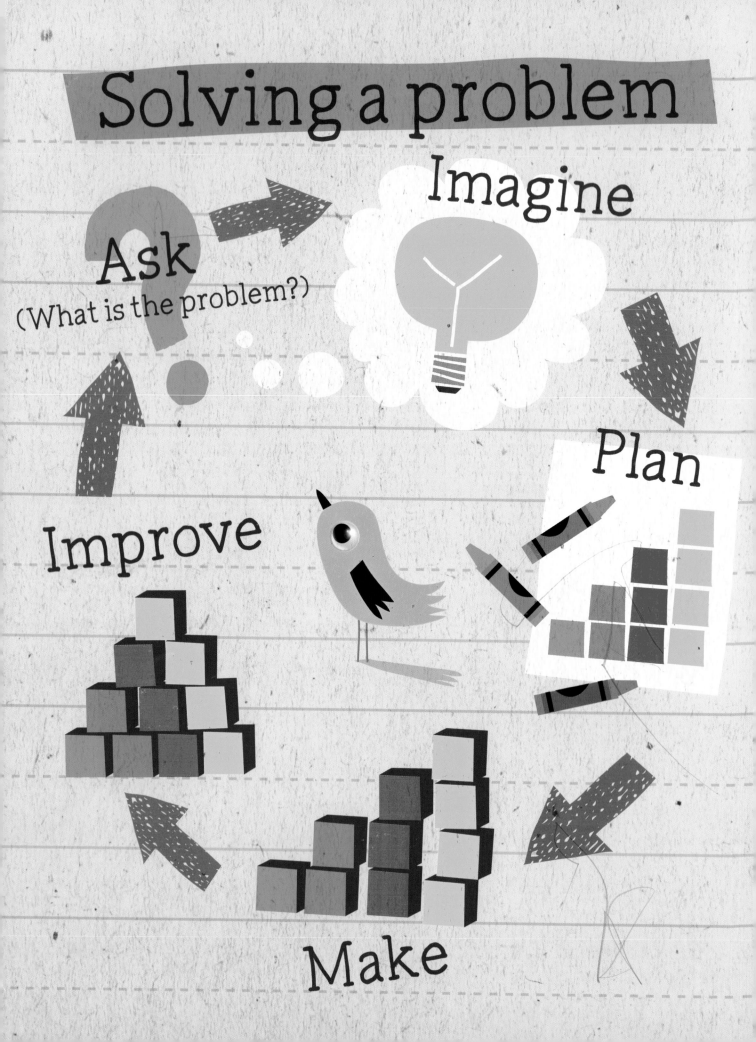